MW01628999

# CARDIOLOGY

## for kids

Dear Keoni and Connor,

Ask questions, stay curious, and never stop learning! You can do anything you put your mind to.

Sincerely,

Dr. Brandon & Dr. Betty

First paperback edition May 2022

Book design by Betty Nguyen & Brandon Pham

ISBN 978-1-957557-03-8 (paperback)
ISBN 978-1-957557-99-1 (hardcover)

Published by Black Phoenix Press



www.mdforkids.org

Disclaimer: Contents of this book are for informational purposes only. No material in this book is intended to provide, or be a substitute for, professional medical advice.

To the friends and family who have supported and loved us unconditionally, and to the mentors who have guided and taught us more than we could have imagined:

**Thank you.**

Betty & Brandon

# Cardiology

(kar-dee-AH-luh-jee)

the branch of medicine concerned with the study and treatment of disorders and diseases of the heart

Place your hand on your chest.
Can you feel your heart beating?

Doctors use a **stethoscope** to listen to the heart. *Lub-dub, lub-dub, lub-dub*!

**No heart murmur**
(valve closes completely)

**Heart murmur**
(valve does not close completely)

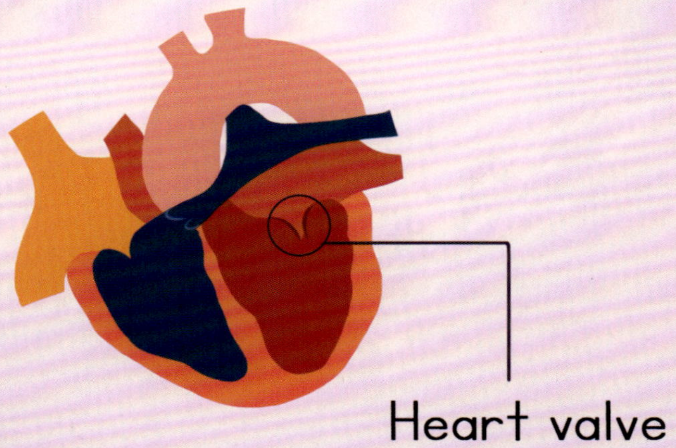


Some people can have an extra humming or whooshing sound between heartbeats. This is called a **heart murmur.**

The heart is structured like a two-story house with four rooms. Each room is called a **chamber**.

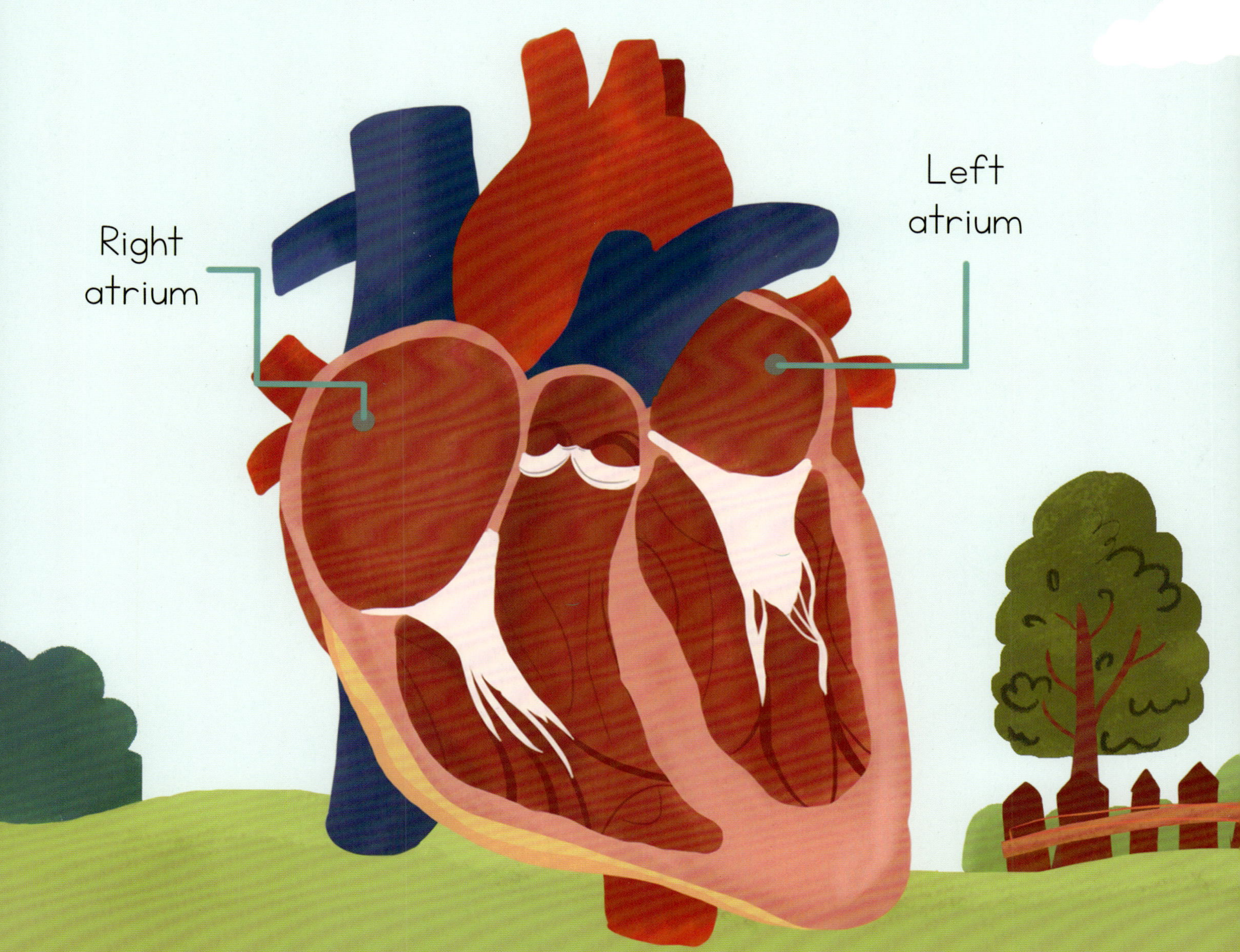


The top two chambers are called **atria**. They are like the two rooms on the top floor of the house.

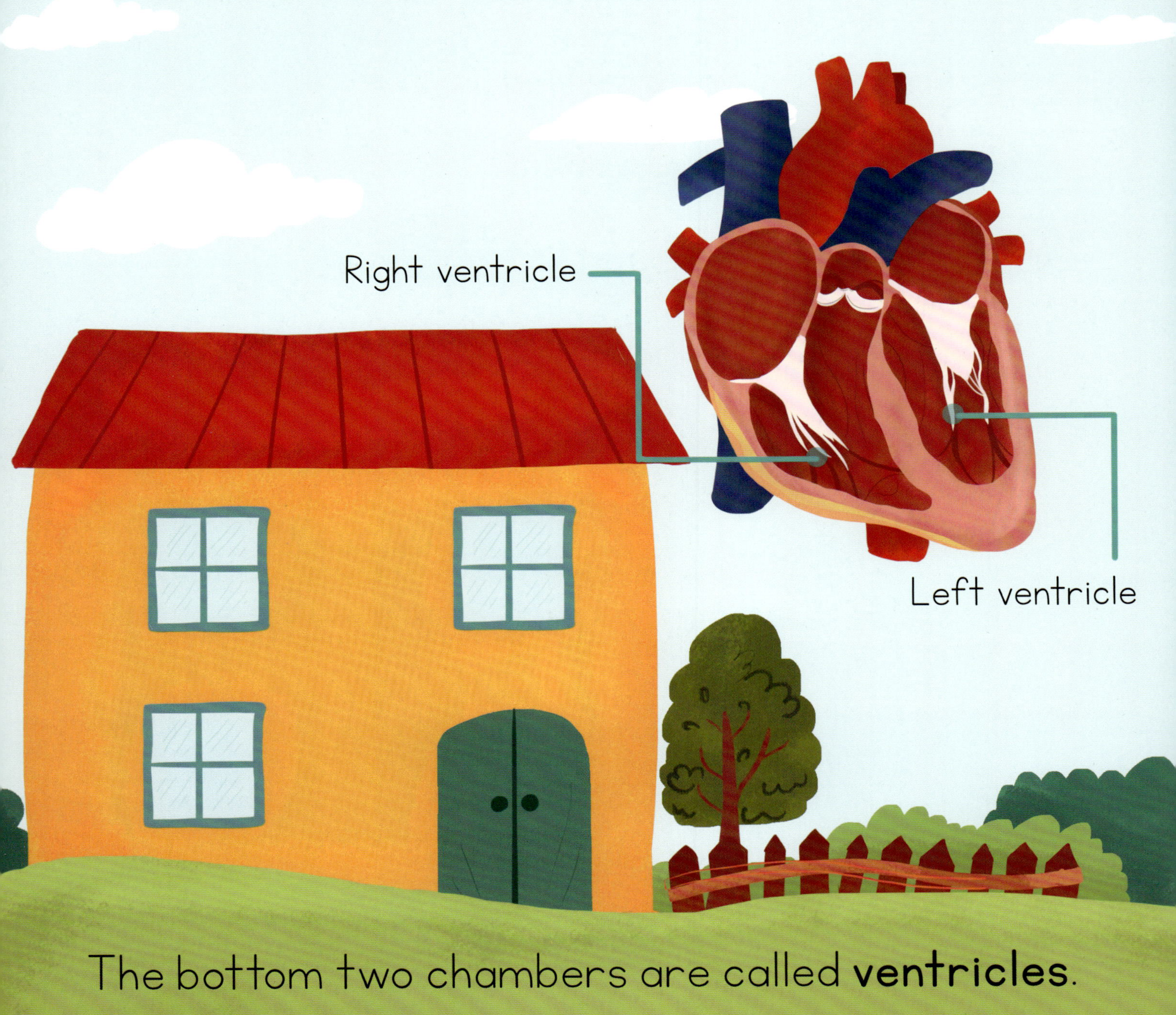


The bottom two chambers are called **ventricles**. They are like the two rooms on the bottom floor.

Have you ever wondered where blood goes in your body with each heartbeat?

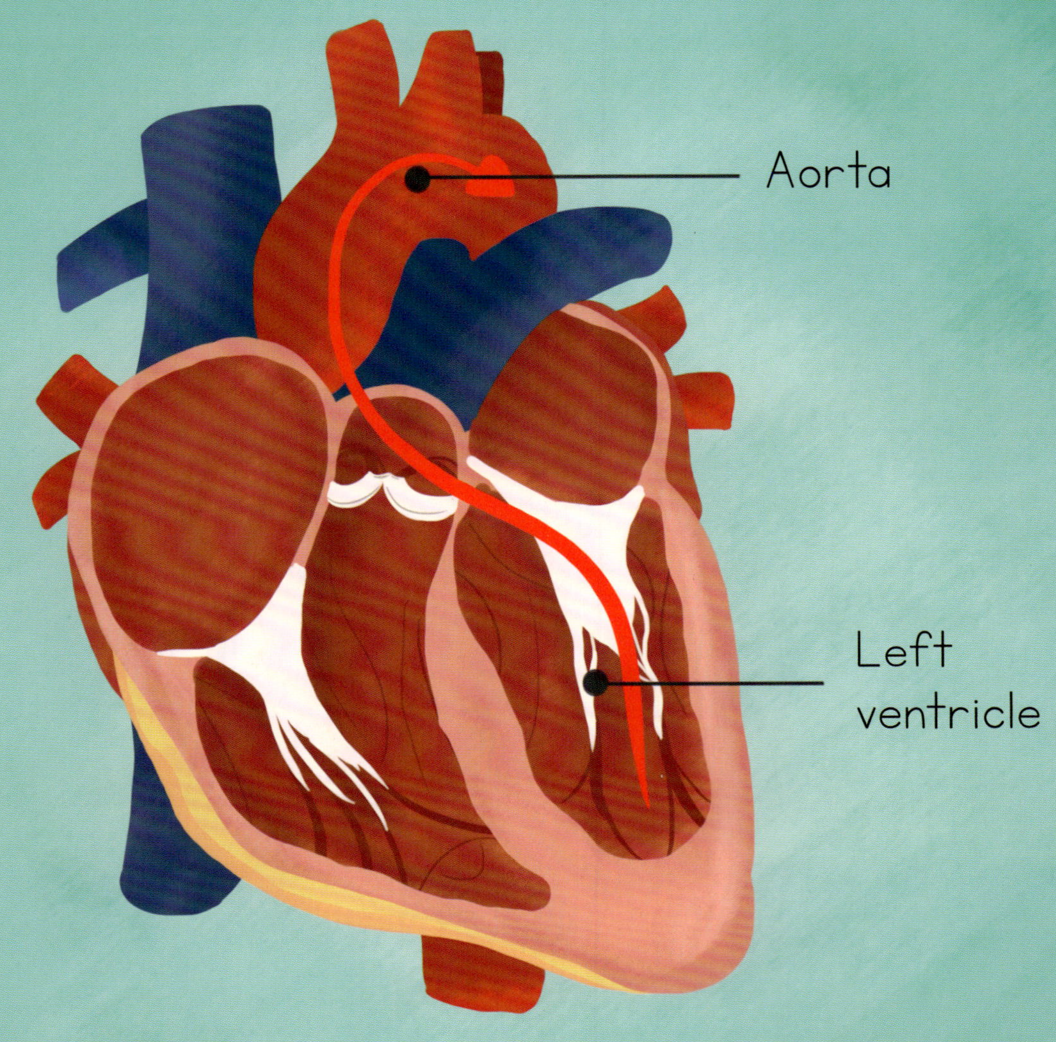


First, the **left ventricle** pumps blood into a big blood vessel called the **aorta**, a type of artery.

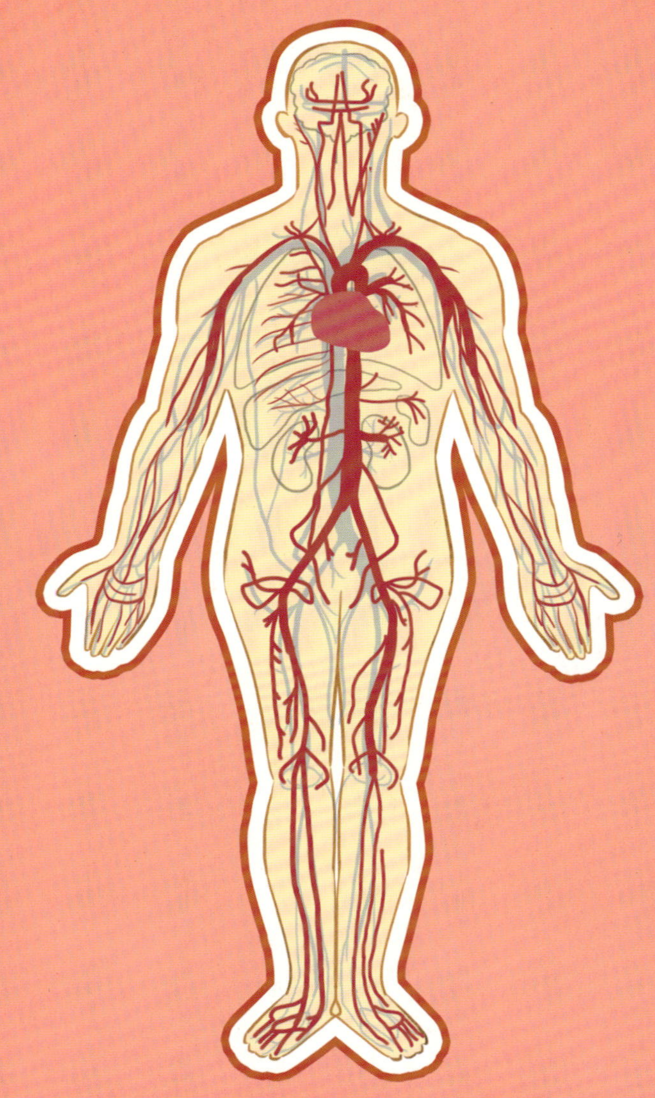

**Arteries** carry blood *away* from the heart to the rest of the body. Most arteries are *high* in oxygen, which our cells need to survive.

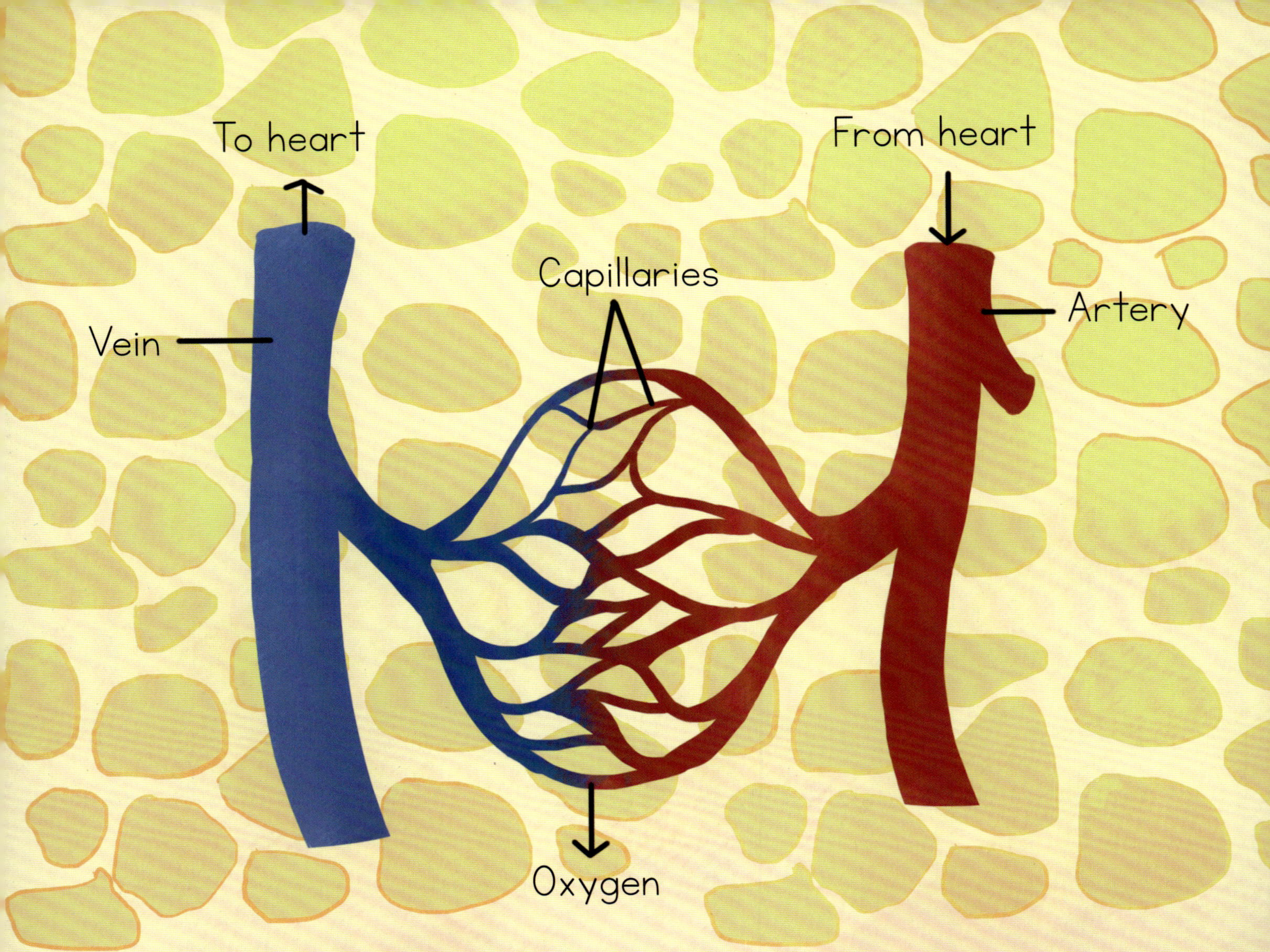


Arteries then branch into **capillaries**. Oxygen moves from capillaries into tissues of the body, which also need oxygen to survive.

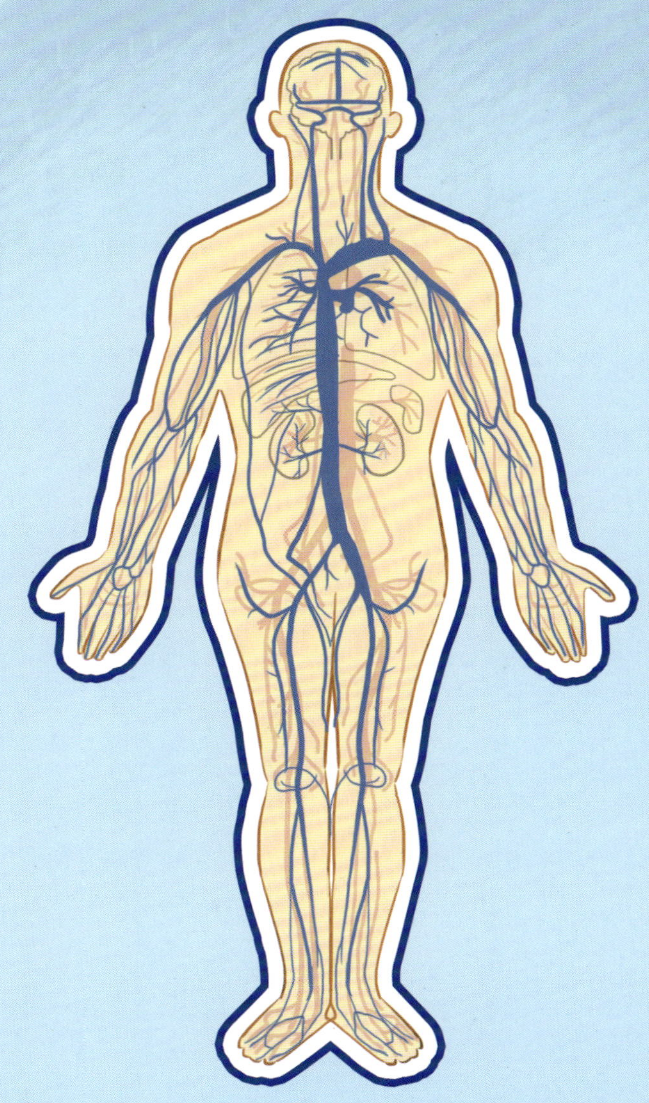

Capillaries then come together to form larger vessels called **veins**. Veins carry blood *toward* the heart. Most veins are *low* in oxygen.

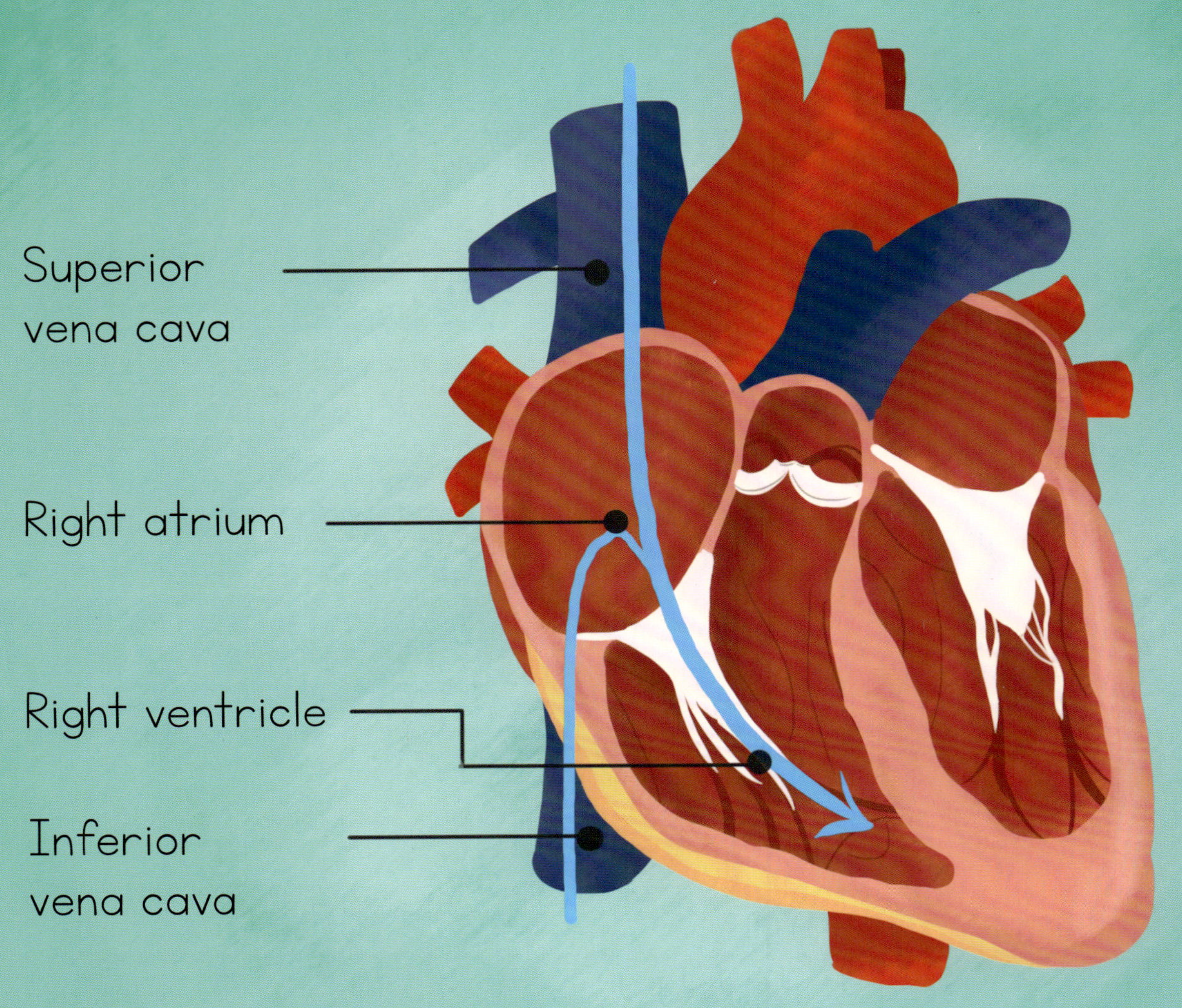


Eventually, all veins come together to form the **vena cava**, which brings blood to the **right atrium** and then **right ventricle**.

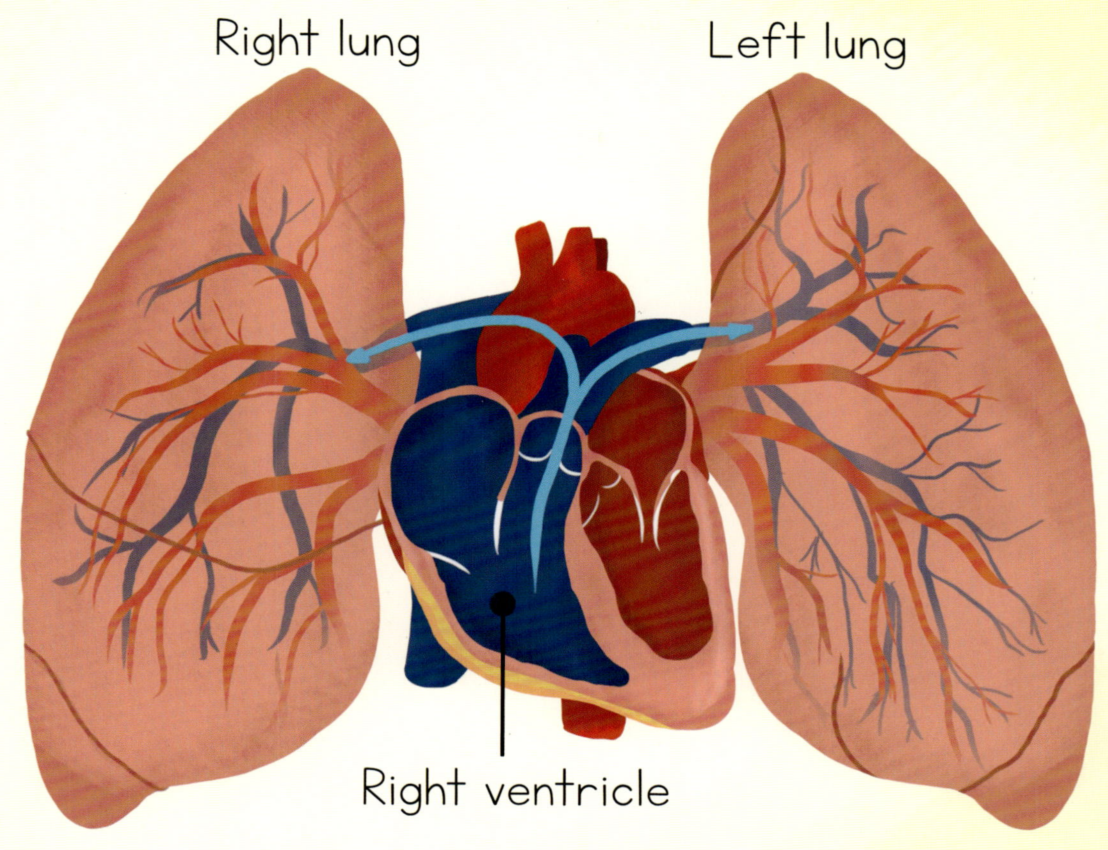


Then, the right ventricle pumps blood to the **lungs,** where blood picks up oxygen from the air we breathe.

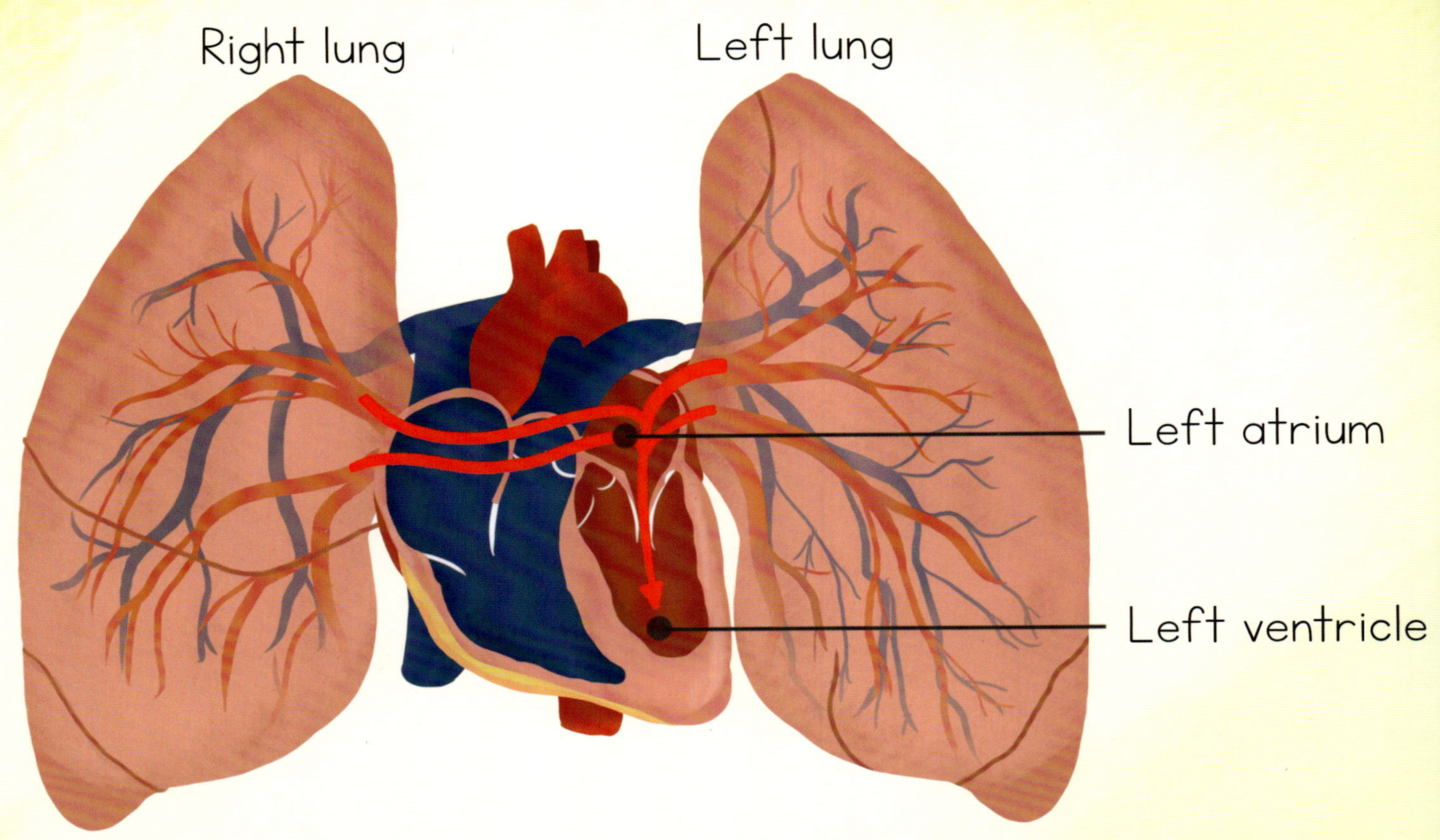


After picking up oxygen in the lungs, blood returns to the **left atrium** and then **left ventricle**. Then, the cycle repeats!

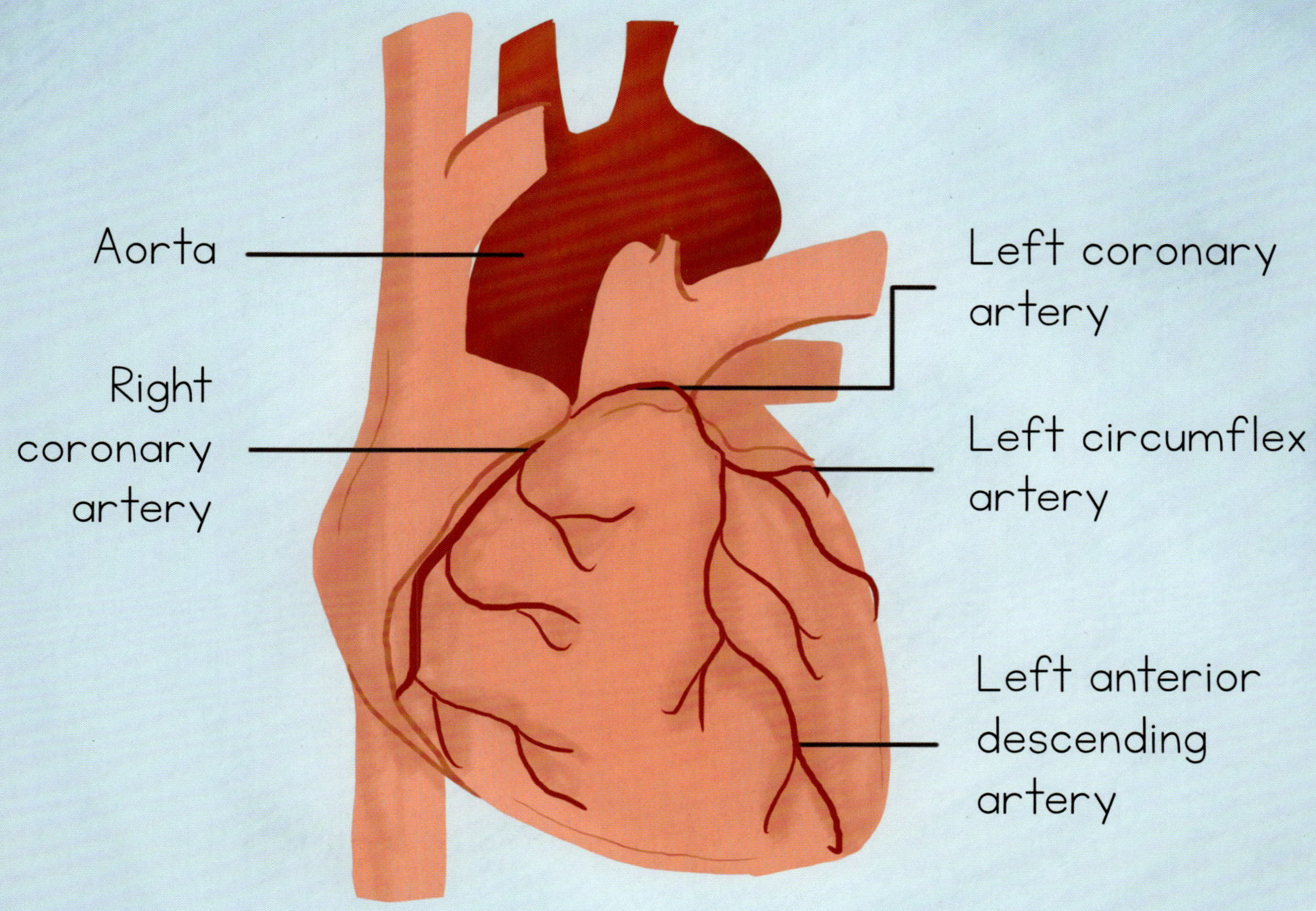


Like the rest of our body, our heart also needs oxygen. **Coronary arteries** supply oxygen to the heart.

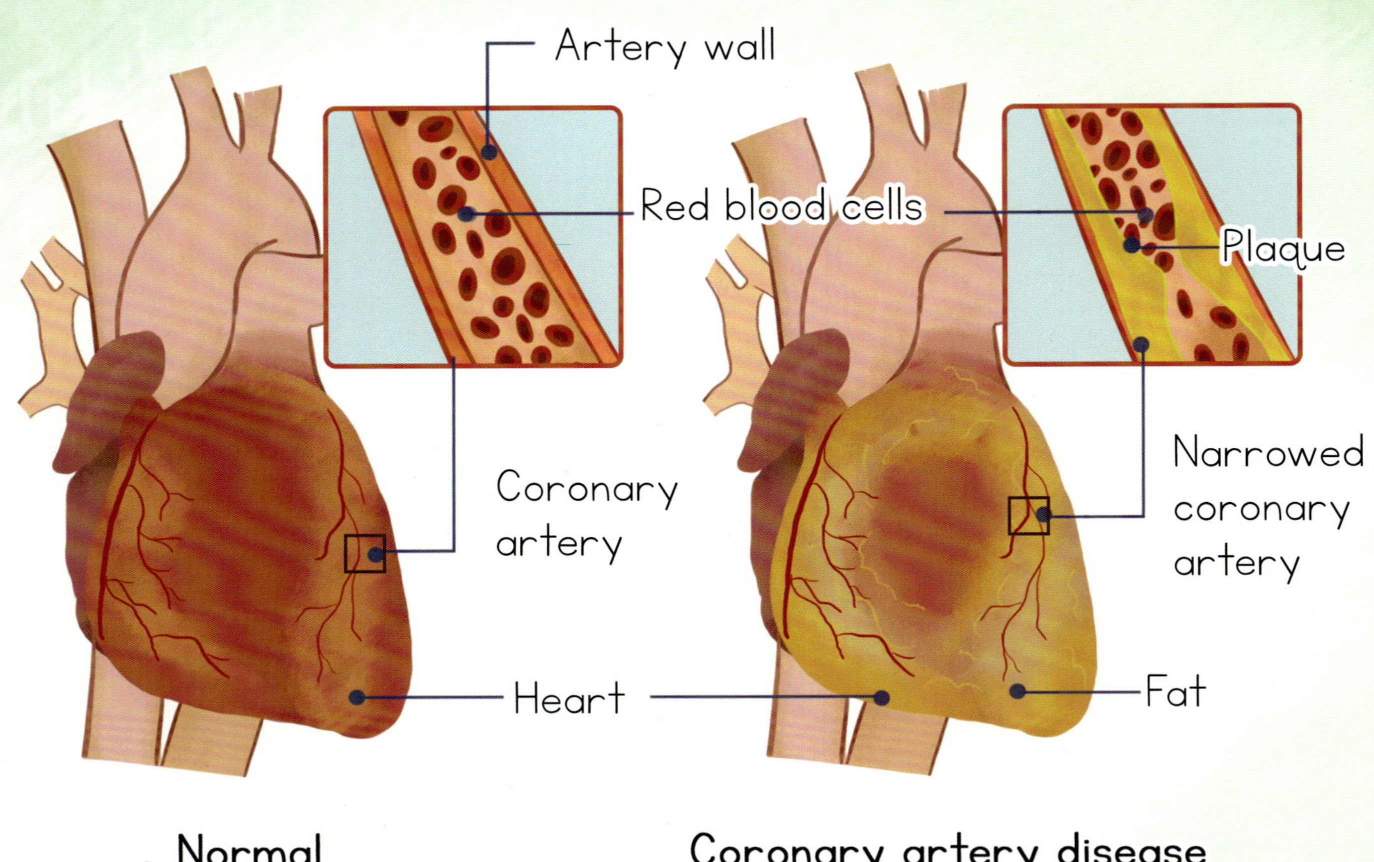


Some people have fatty deposits in their coronary arteries that reduce blood flow to the heart. This is called **coronary artery disease.**

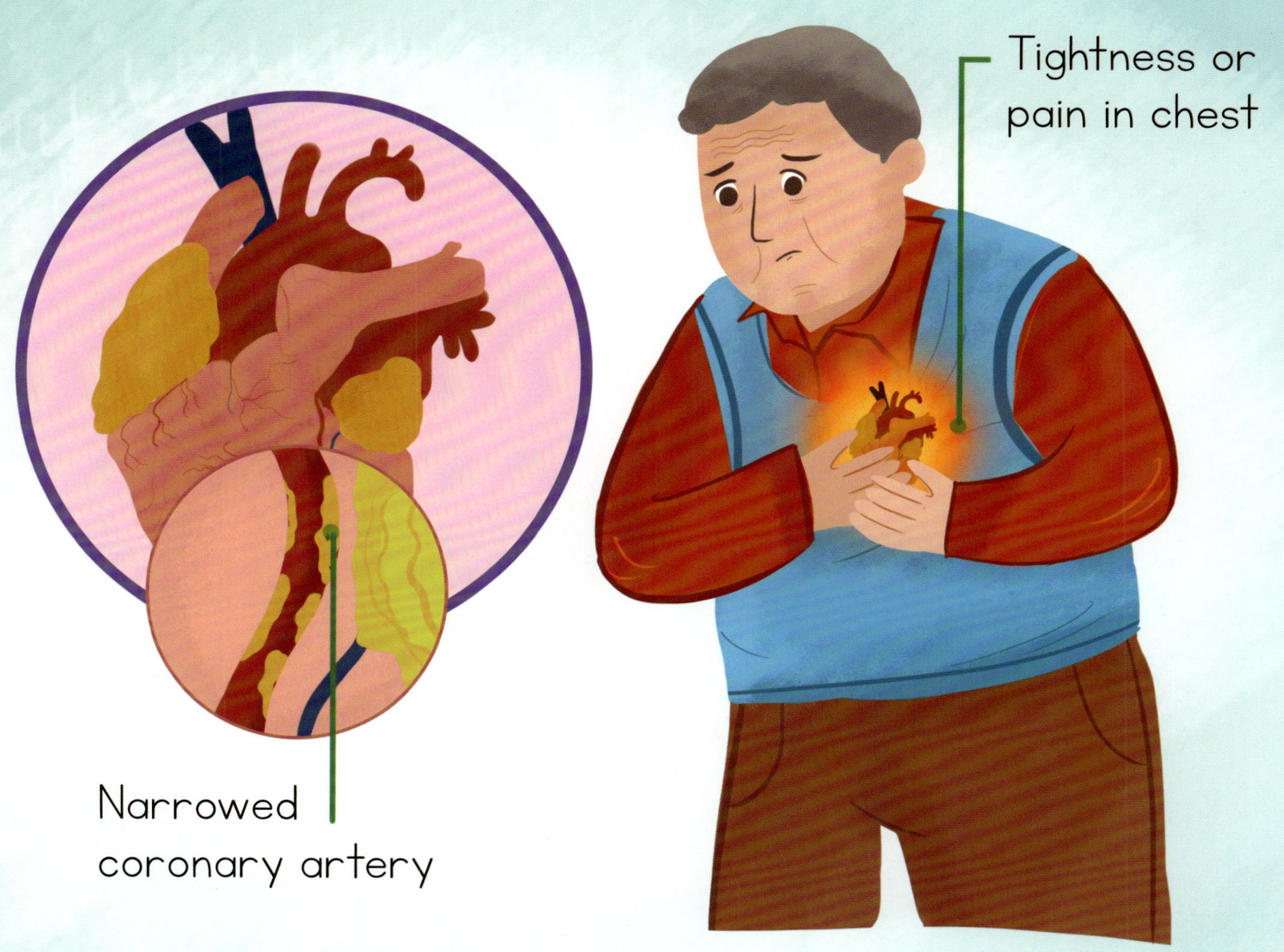


If the heart does not get enough oxygen, a person can feel chest pain. This is called **angina**.

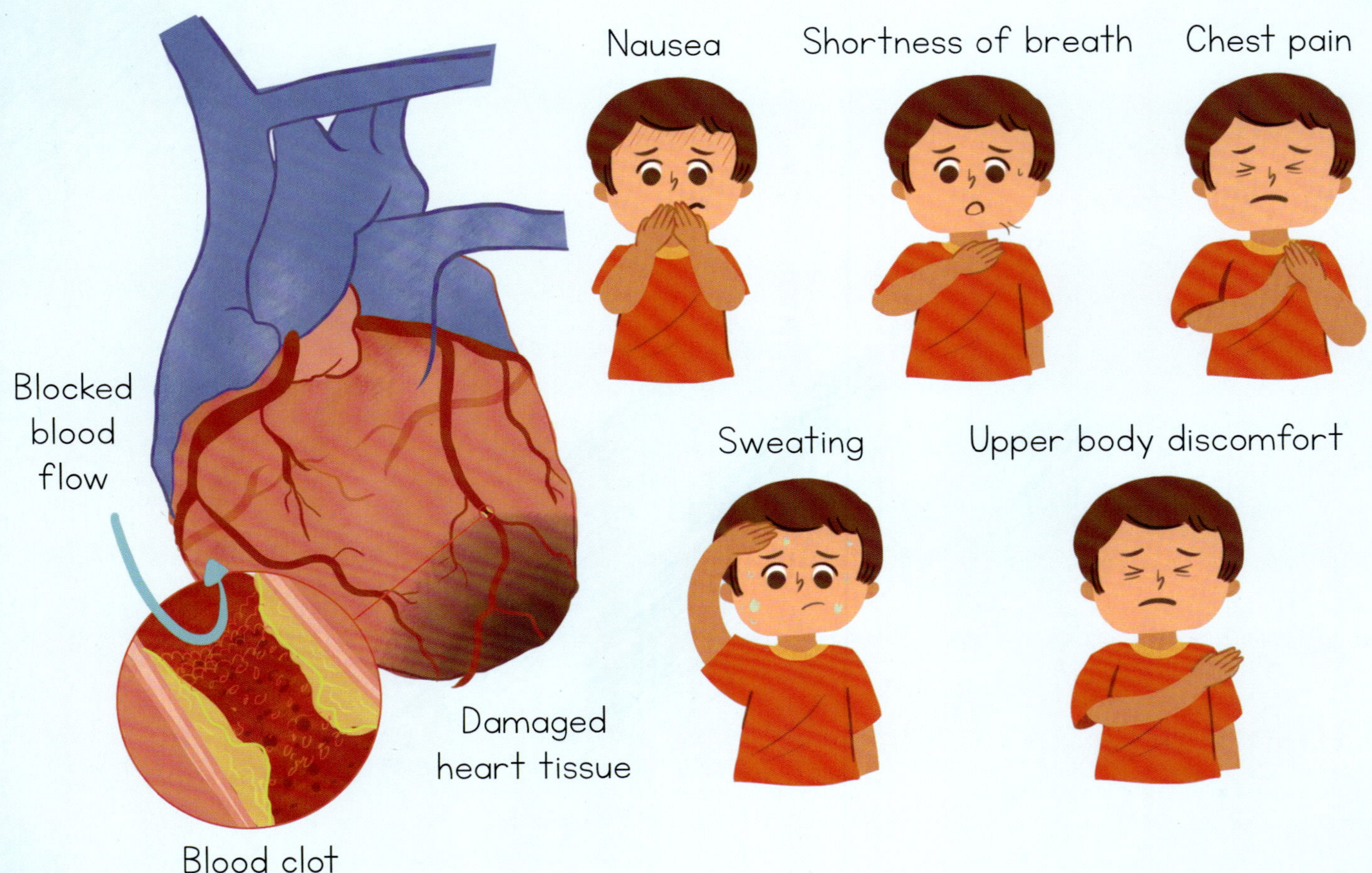


If a coronary artery is completely blocked, a section of the heart can't get enough oxygen and will be damaged. This is called a **heart attack**.

A person having a heart attack needs to go to the hospital right away. Call 911 if you think someone is having a heart attack.

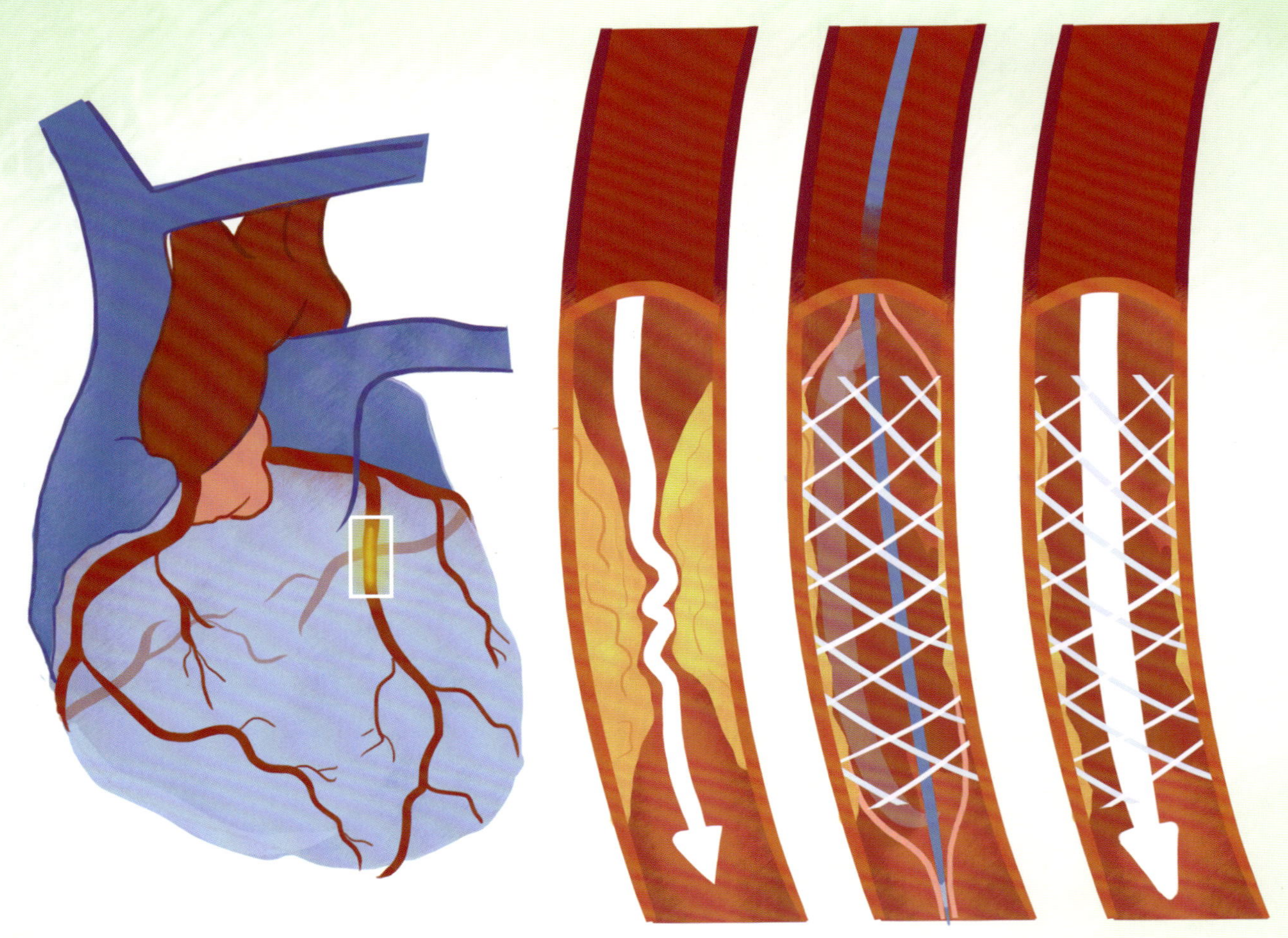

Doctors can open the blocked coronary artery with a tiny balloon and keep it open with a small expandable mesh. This is called **coronary angioplasty** and **stenting**.

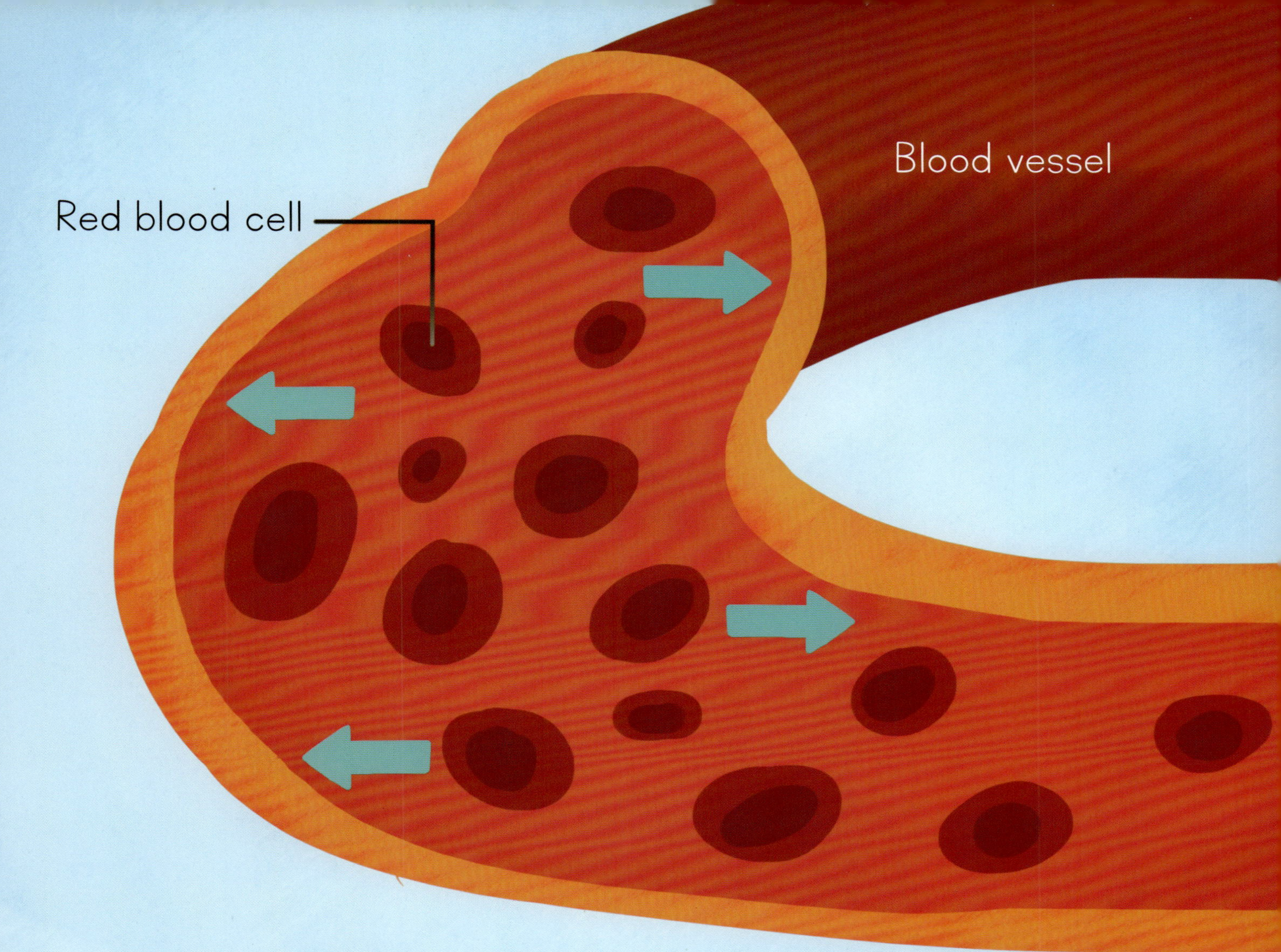


As blood flows throughout our body, it pushes against the walls of arteries. This is called **blood pressure**.

Doctors can measure your blood pressure with a **sphygmomanometer**. A normal blood pressure helps keep your heart healthy.

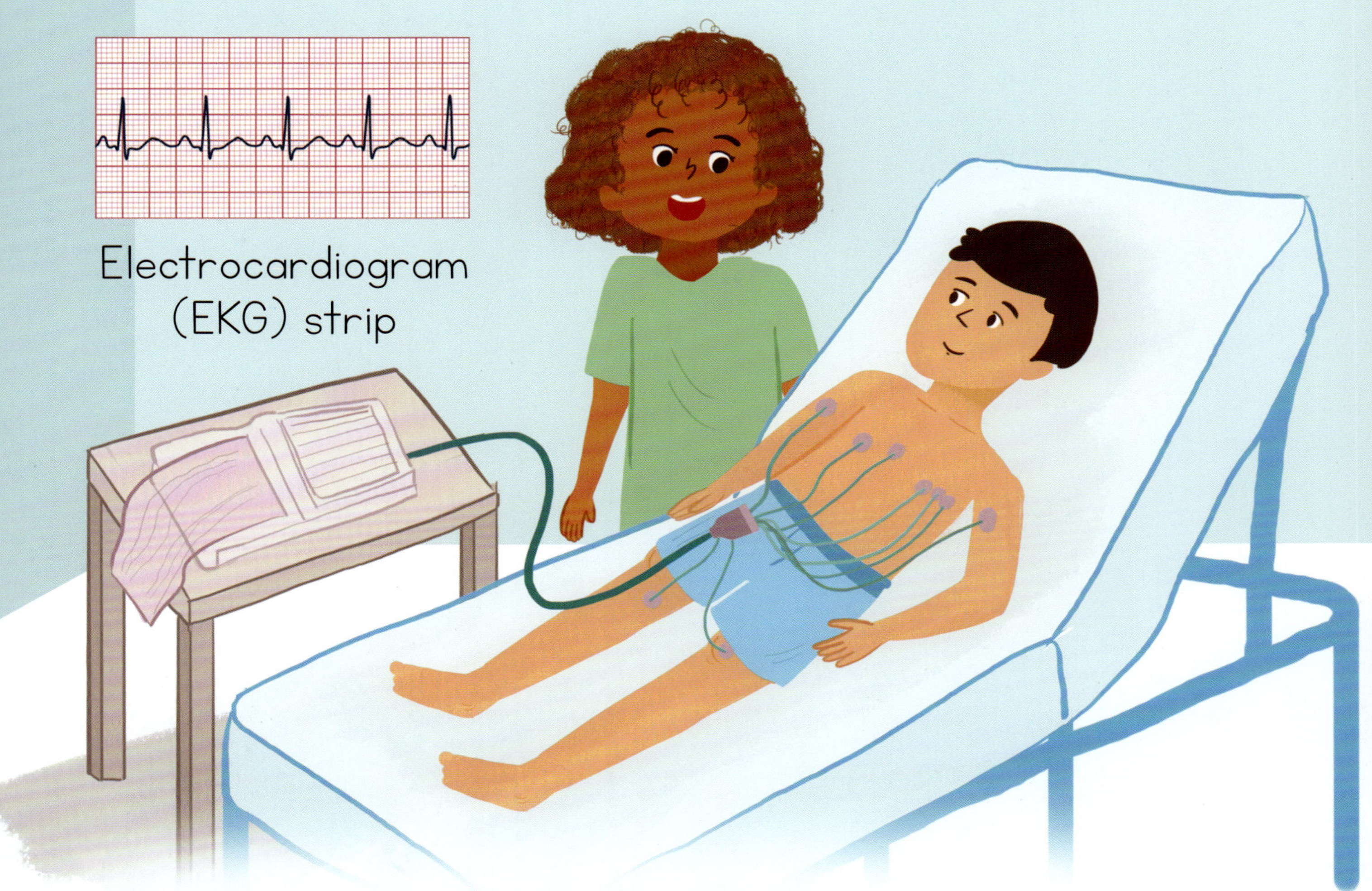


Our heart has an electrical system that coordinates each heartbeat. Doctors measure this electrical activity with an **electrocardiogram.**

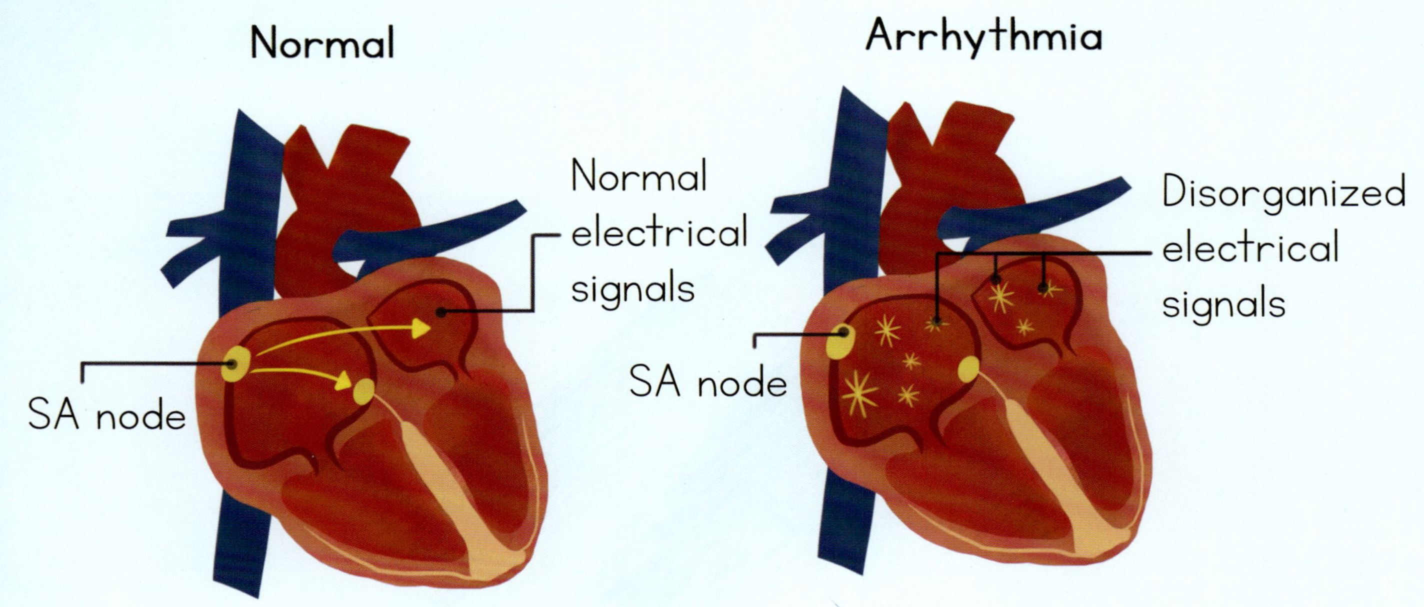


An EKG can be used to find out if someone has an abnormal or irregular heartbeat. This is called an **arrhythmia**.

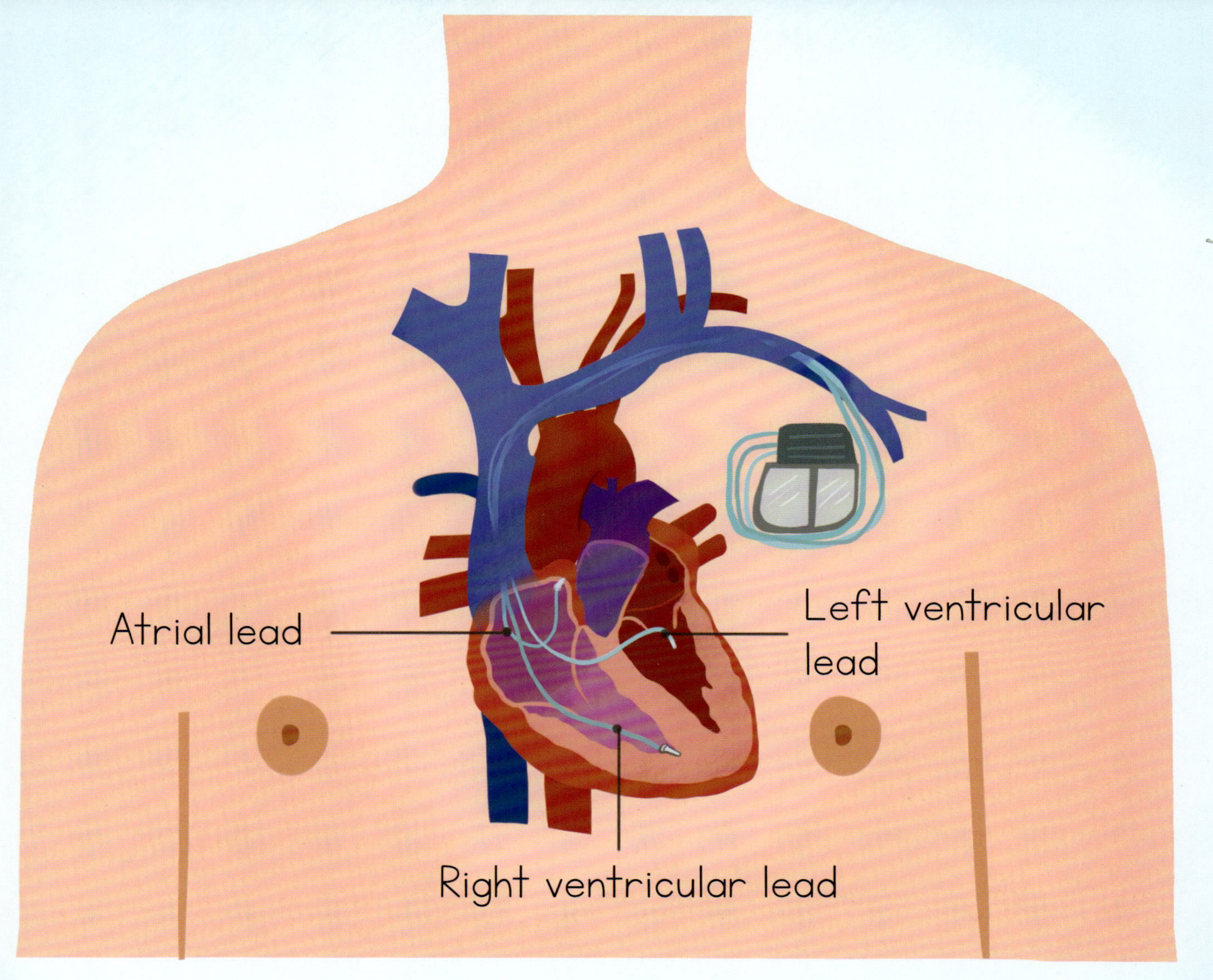


Some people with arrhythmias need a **pacemaker**, which is a small electronic device placed inside the chest that helps control their heartbeat.

Doctors can also measure how well the heart pumps blood with an **echocardiogram**, which creates pictures of the heart using sound waves.

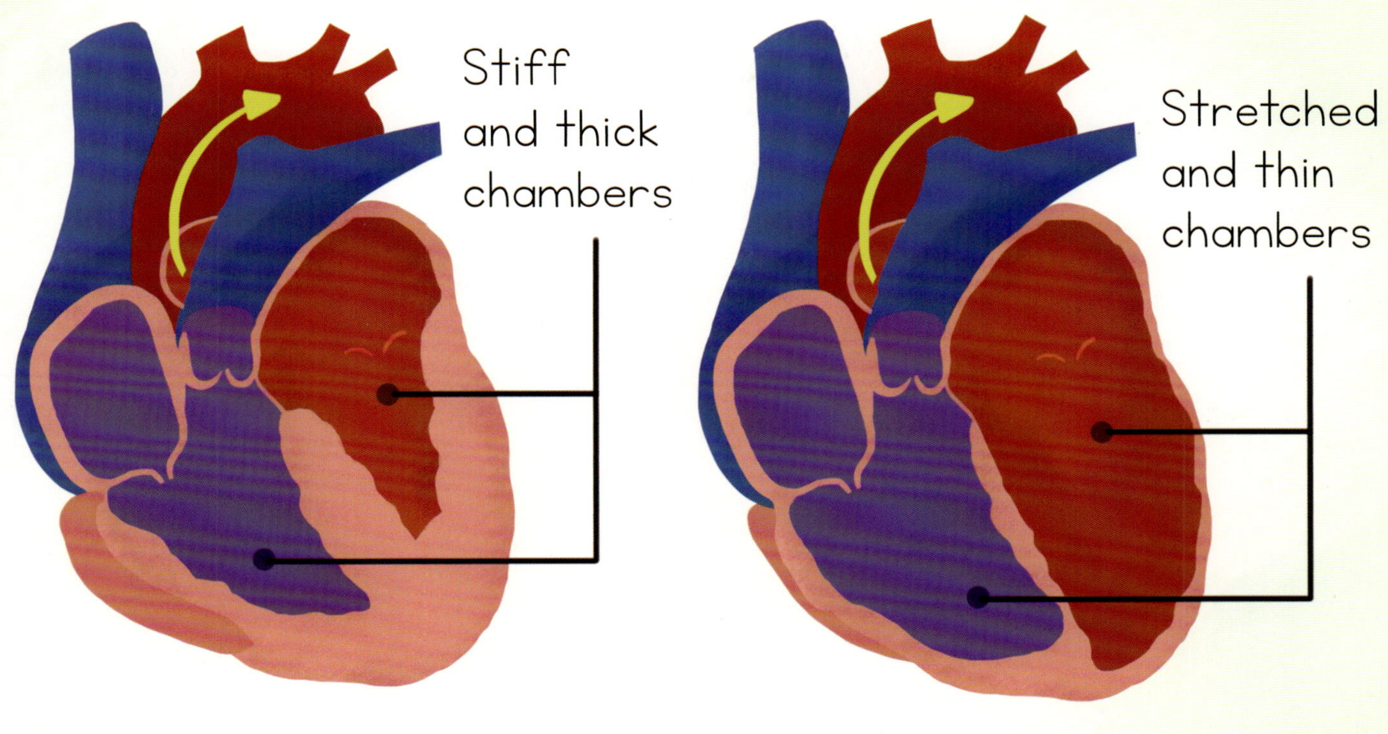


An echocardiogram can be used to diagnose **congestive heart failure**, which occurs if the heart can't pump or fill with blood normally.

Fortunately, patients with congestive heart failure can take medications to improve symptoms and live longer, healthier lives.

Your heart is a very important organ. Eating healthy foods and exercising regularly can keep your heart healthy.

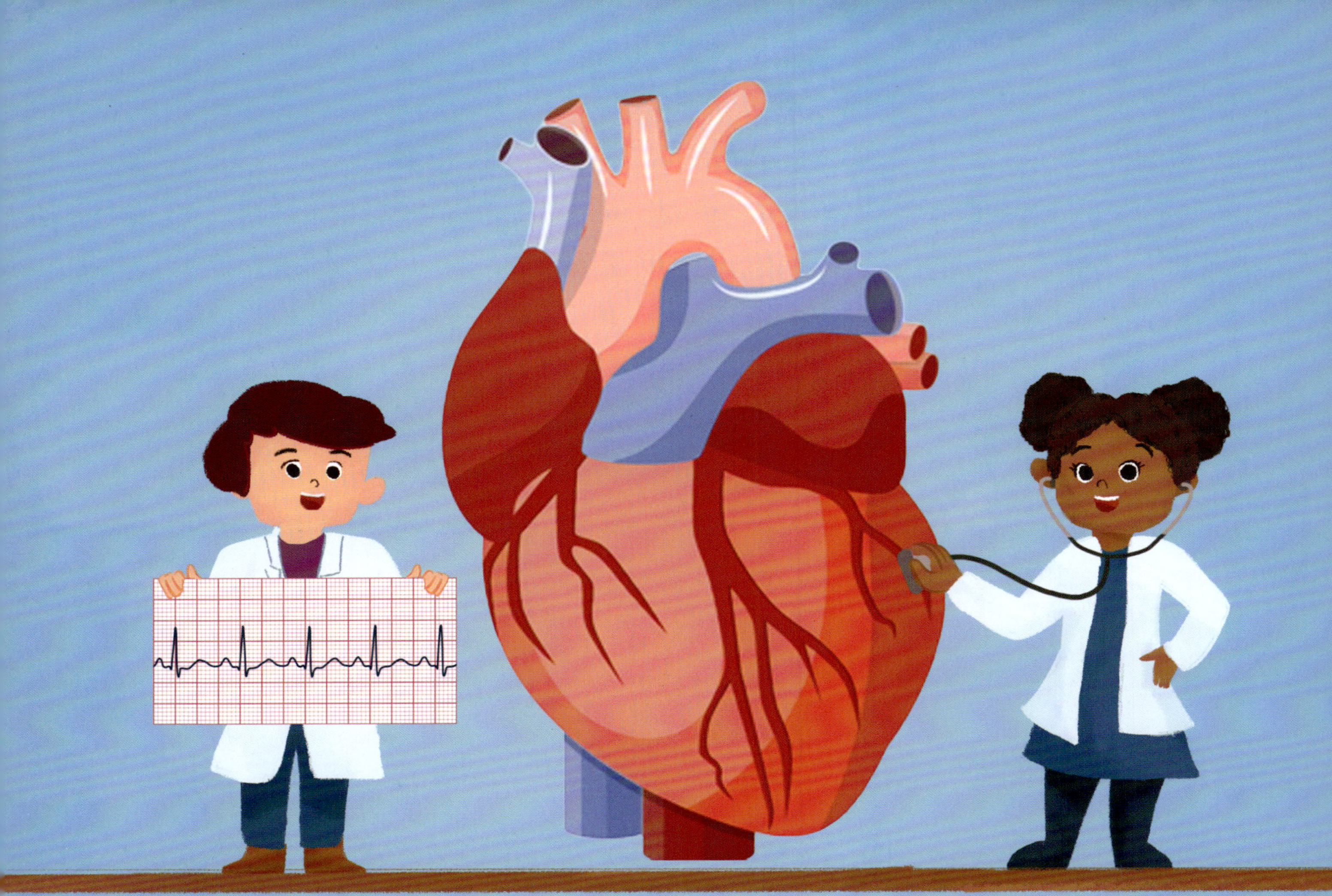

YOU'RE A FUTURE CARDIOLOGIST!

# Glossary

**Angina** (an-JAI-nuh): chest pain caused by ↓ blood supply to the heart
**Arrhythmia** (ur-ITH-mee-uh): abnormal or irregular heartbeat
**Atria** (AY-tree-uh): top 2 chambers of the heart that *receive* blood
**Blood pressure**: amount of force that blood "pushes" against the walls of arteries as it flows throughout our body
**Congestive heart failure**: condition in which the heart does not pump (systolic) or fill (diastolic) with blood normally
**Coronary artery disease** (KAW-ruh-neh-ree): buildup of fatty deposits in the coronary arteries, causing reduced blood flow to the heart
**Coronary angioplasty and stenting** (AN-jee-uh-pla-stee): surgical procedure in which doctors open a blocked coronary artery with a tiny balloon and keep it open with a small expandable mesh
**Echocardiogram**: test that creates pictures of the heart using sound waves
**Electrocardiogram**: test that measures electrical activity of the heart
**Heart attack**: sudden blockage of a coronary artery, causing a section of the heart to lack oxygen and become damaged
**Murmur** (MUR-mr): extra humming or whooshing sound between heartbeats
**Pacemaker**: small electronic device placed inside the chest that helps control the heartbeat; also called a cardiac pacing device
**Sphygmomanometer** (sfig-mow-muh-NAA-muh-tr): device used to measure blood pressure, usually used in conjunction with a stethoscope
**Ventricles** (VEN-truh-klz): bottom 2 chambers of the heart that *pump* blood

# Let's review what you learned!

1. What medical instrument do doctors use to listen to the heart?
2. What is an extra humming or whooshing sound between heartbeats called?
3. What are the 4 chambers of the heart?
4. Where does the left ventricle pump blood to?
5. What are differences between arteries and veins? What are capillaries?
6. What blood vessel brings blood to the right atrium?
7. Where does the right ventricle pump blood to?
8. After blood receives oxygen from the lungs, where does it go?
9. What are the blood vessels that supply oxygen to the hecrt called?
10. People with fatty deposits in their coronary arteries have what disease?
11. What is chest pain caused by a heart not getting enough oxygen called?
12. What is a heart attack? How is it treated?
13. What is an electrocardiogram? What condition can it help diagnose?
14. What is a pacemaker?
15. What is an echocardiogram? What condition can it help diagnose?

# Your Answers

1. ______________________________
2. ______________________________
3. ______________________________
4. ______________________________
5. ______________________________
6. ______________________________
7. ______________________________
8. ______________________________
9. ______________________________
10. ______________________________
11. ______________________________
12. ______________________________
13. ______________________________
14. ______________________________
15. ______________________________

# Answer Key

1. Stethoscope
2. Heart murmur
3. Right atrium, right ventricle, left atrium, left ventricle
4. To the rest of the body through the aorta (largest artery in the body)
5. Arteries carry blood away from the heart and are usually high in oxygen; veins carry blood toward the heart and are usually low in oxygen; capillaries are tiny blood vessels that connect arteries with veins
6. Vena cava (largest vein in the body)
7. To the lungs (through the pulmonary artery)
8. To the left atrium and then left ventricle (through the pulmonary veins)
9. Coronary arteries
10. Coronary artery disease
11. Angina
12. Condition caused by a completely blocked coronary artery; treated with coronary angioplasty and stenting
13. Test that measures electrical activity of the heart; arrhythmia
14. Electronic device placed inside the chest to help control the heartbeat
15. Test that creates pictures of the heart using sound waves; heart failure

# About the Authors

## Betty Nguyen

Betty Nguyen was born in California but spent much of her childhood in Georgia, where she grew up on a chicken farm. She received a bachelor's degree in Biology from UCLA, where she received a full-ride Gates Millennium Scholarship through the Bill & Melinda Gates Foundation. Betty also received a full-tuition scholarship to attend medical school at the University of California, Riverside. Outside of work, Betty is a certified yoga instructor and licensed scuba diver. She also enjoys journalistic writing, cycling, and walking her two dogs in her free time.

## Brandon Pham

Brandon Pham was born and raised in California. He received a bachelor's degree in Microbiology, Immunology, and Molecular Genetics from UCLA, where he was a national Goldwater Scholar. He graduated from Stanford Medical School and is currently completing his residency in ophthalmology at the Bascom Palmer Eye Institute in Miami, Florida. Brandon spent many years teaching for several national test-preparation companies and is passionate about medical education for students of all ages. In his free time, Brandon enjoys traveling, playing tennis, and distance running.

# Check out the rest of the books in our series!

Website: mdforkids.org

Instagram: @md.for.kids